site with the drumming and singing. To me, this was both a celebration and a mystical experience. The pipes, the mist, the whole atmosphere of the place transported up to the realm of myth and magic, and I broke through personal barriers and opened new doorways for myself. As I watched the sparks fly into the air from the last embers of the Wicker Man, I knew our offerings had been accepted, and that the coming year will be a fruitful one for our community. This was a once in a lifetime experience that I will treasure for ever.

The Origins of the Word Witch
by R.J. Thompson

The origin of the English "witch" may be the Indo-European (IE) root word weik, having to deal with magic and/or religion. From weik we get four different derivatives of the word. The first derivative is the word wih-l, which in turn begat the Old English words wigle and wiglera, meaning sorcery and sorcerer respectively. These words are also the root of the word guile. The second derivative is similar in spelling to the first and is the Old Norse wihl, meaning craftiness. The third is wik, meaning holy. From wik comes the Middle High German wich, having the same meaning as its root word, derived itself from the Old High German wihen. The fourth derivative of the word is wikk, meaning magic or sorcery. From this comes the Middle German wikken, meaning to predict. Wikk also begat the Old English wicca and wicce (respectively pronounced wee-cha and wee-chay, roughly, I am no linguist.) These words pertaining to a practice comparable to Seidr, wicca being the masculine variant and wicce the female. From these words is the verb wician, roughly meaning to work sorcery. Wicca then begat the Middle English witche and from this our modern witch.

It should be stated that if one wishes to practice what can truly be called witchcraft it will be a mystical path of Germanic, or at the least IE, origin. This is not to say that it will be of a pure strand of Germanic or IE based paganism, as true traditional craft would vary from locale to locale and pick up many magio/spiritual practices along the way. Nor is modern witchcraft called "wicca" necessarily "witchcraft." This is not to say that modern wicca is not a valid path and religion, but it is wicca, not witchcraft in a traditional sense. Much of modern "witchcraft" and wicca is derived from ceremonial practices, such as those of the Golden Dawn. While this is fine by itself, it was something of the unknown to the practitioners of wicca (Saxon usage,) a Germanic path.

As a final note I will discuss the idea that wicca is a word that means to bend or to shape. This idea has its root in fact, to a point. The Old English word (no doubt derived from the same root as those words discussed above) wican, did, indeed, mean to bend. Related words are the Old Saxon wikan, the Old High German wichan and the Old Norse vikja. All of these words having the meaning to bend.

It may also be noted that the practice of traditional wicca and wicce (Saxon uses here) and Medieval Witchcraft (the origins of the craft in many of the forms that we know it) are derived from Galdr and Seidr (mentioned above) and are the Saxon variants of these. Thus the path of the Helrunar and the Haegtessa are far closer to Traditional Witchcraft than most modern "Craft." "Witchcraft" in it's origin was very much a religion, first and foremost, and it's practitioners were "mystics" and "shamans" in a sense. This should be noted, for folk magic and witchcraft are not one in the same, as believed by many, though the former is practiced by those of the persuasion of the latter. Nor are modern wicca and old craft truly the same, as believed by others. That said, modern traditional witchcraft only bears a passing semblance to what would have passed for craft in times before. And that, as they say, is that.

Unless otherwise stated, all text in within this article is original and Copyright © 2007 by R.J. Thompson. All images used in this document are in the public domain.

Witch's Ritual for Getting Rid of Evil Magic – "Ku Potula"

by Radomir Ristic

In Serbian territory and in the Balkans also, there is a tradition that many people turn to Witches for help when they suspect that some magical attack is performed against them, attacks which they cannot resist as individuals. These people are not only from rural communities but could be citizens from all social strata. Help from the Witches, who mainly lives in rural areas, could be requested by housewives from the villages and cities but also employed people, doctors, people with a college education, and politicians. Of course, when people in high places are involved in something like this, it must be kept secret, and that cannot become known.

The reason why these people think they are the target of some magical attack lies in the fact that our tradition actually includes these practices. Some people, because of their strong desire to get even for something, or to cause damage or some evil to their business rival, to their fighting neighbor, or to some person who is their competitor for some job, contact an appropriate Witch who is specialized in certain evil actions, and request her to hurt someone in a magical way. People must pay for these services. Although the number of these Witches is small, they do exist. This is not about some special system of black magic, but of the use of regular magic for the purpose of evil. This means that good and evil Witches use the same magical system but in different ways. In brief, both contact the same entities but they demand different things from them. Some of them want to cure somebody, and some of them want that somebody becomes ill. Some of them demand business success for a certain person, and some of them want to ruin someone financially. In either case, the entities contacted are very neutral and they simply carry out the will of the Witch that contacts them. Essentially everyone has the power to make contact with these entities, and to do whatever they want to. That is why there is no black and white magic in the Balkans but only good and bad Witches.

For causing damage to somebody, people usually contact water spirits, or make a magical potion (for example, the potion could be made of the water in which a deceased man had been bathed). A skull of some "bad" animal can be used - a rag doll must be run through its jaws, and this rag doll symbolizes the person for whom the magic is intended. Very often people use an egg that represents a symbol of life, which is named after the intended victim, and becomes that person with their living strength. It is especially interesting that in these rituals no one contacts the Devil or some evil demon per se. People sometimes contact the Devil for good things, when nothing else could help, because people think that he can remove any evil. But evil demons should never be contacted, because they do not have any special powers but being what they are. For the same purposes, people contact Forest Mother, Water Mother, Great Water spirit, fairies, etc. Spirits of ancestors should not be contacted for evil things, because they don't want to do such things, and they have their own attitude about that in contrast to spirits of nature and deities, which are neutral.

Still, these evil Witches often have limits that they don't want to pass. It is very hard to find one who will want to do everything. It is very interesting that they don't want to perform rituals for hurting someone arbitrarily. The reason for this lies in the fact that they all believe in some sort of karma, not in exactly the same way as India's people do, but quite similar. They believe that they will have a guilty conscience and that they will suffer when they die. Because of this, they warn all their clients about it, and they perform the ritual only if the client agrees that everything done will be the client's responsibility. Each ritual they begin with following words:

"Everything I do is responsibility of (name of the client)"

In contrast to these people, others turn to Witches for help to get rid of evil magic that was cast on them. Any Witch, even the one who cast spells on somebody under the direction of her clients, could perform those rituals. Even more, many people turn to those Witches for help because they think they know best what could be happening to them.

One question raised here is how those people who came to the Witches know that somebody cast spells on them? There are two factors involved. The first one is their state of health, and the second one is good luck or, better to say, bad luck in their life. Namely, if somebody notices that their state of health is getting worse and doctors cannot determine some valid cause for this state, the first thing that person is going to think is that someone cast spells on them. Here we can include depression, insomnia, and loss of appetite, unwillingness, nightmares, and similar things. When it is about luck, usually the person notices that nothing works for them properly, that they cannot get a promotion, that they lose their job in an odd way, that their girlfriend or boyfriend leave them with no obvious reason, that people starts to avoid them, that they fall often and that accidents in house become frequent, etc.

When person notices something like that, they want to find a Witch, often recommended by a neighbor, co-worker, or some other acquaintance. As a rule, people want the most successful one. They visit the Witch, who tries to find out whether someone cast spells on them, or if it is something else. If she confirms that the suspicions of the client are justified, she resorts to performing one of many rituals for that purpose.

For this article, we have selected one very old ritual from Eastern Serbia; it was performed in the territory where Serbs and Vlachs live together from ancient times. The name of this ancient ritual is preserved, thanks to the fact that people still perform it: "Ku potula" in the Vlach language, and it can be performed in the following way.

When some person asks a Witch for help, that first day the witch goes to the closest river or stream and takes white stones from there. She takes the same number of stones as the number of the steps the stairs from the bottom to the entrance. That means, if there are four steps, she will take out four white stones. These stones should represent water spirits or, to be precise, the Great Water Spirit named Tartor. Vlach people consider the white stone as a symbol of chthonic forces and it can represent Tartor and Lusjafur. In those areas, people still put white stone in the pocket of deceased person before closing the coffin. After she has done that, she goes back home. She begins to perform the ritual on that day that is matched with the number of steps to entrance, so that the last day of performing the ritual must be Tuesday. This means that if there are four steps, she will begin to perform the ritual on Saturday. The first time she will do it on Saturday, the second time on Sunday, the third time on Monday and, finally, the fourth time in Tuesday. On the first day, she will put one white stone on the first step. She will step on it and she will press it down with her feet, moving her feet left and right. While she does that, she holds a kerchief in her hand that is raised over her head and waving with it on four sides of the world. After that, while her feet are still on that white stone, she lowers the kerchief with both hands, and while looking it she will pronounce following incantation:

"Steady, steady horse above all other horses; exert all strength to calm down the entire empire. Steady, steady, just like you calm down cows in stables, pigs in pigsties, sheep in sheepfolds, hens in chicken cops, dogs in kennels, people in the villages … in the same way you calm down J.D. too ".

After she repeats that three times, the witch ties a knot in the kerchief. She repeats this three times, tying three knots in total. With this act, all cast spells and intentions are tied up. The next morning, the witch will untie these three knots, whose magic is weaker in the morning, and she will repeat this four days in a row, and the last time on the last step on Tuesday. After that, she will do all this again simultaneously on all four steps in Thursday and Saturday. She chooses these days because they are considered very favorable days for performing magical acts. However, these days aren't obligated for everybody. In another tradition in that same area people think the good days are Monday, Wednesday, and Sunday. The thing that is the same in these two cases is existence of the belief that three days in the week are favorable for performing magical acts. At the end, the person for whom this ritual was performed visits the witch on Saturday and the witch gives them the ritual kerchief that is untied but it is considered filled with magical energy. To the person to which she gives the kerchief, the witch orders them to sleep with it, whether they will put it around their head or under the pillow, until next Tuesday when this person will come back again to determine whether the magic was successful or not. If the results are negative, another ritual must be performed but it must be a stronger and more dramatic one.

Tapping The Bone

by Peter Paddon

Many cultures around the world operate from a belief that the Gods are divine ancestors, from the Shinto religion in Japan, through many African traditions and the Maoris, to many of the Witchcraft Traditions of old Europe. For most of them, reverence for more mundane ancestors is also a major factor in their beliefs.

As a practitioner of the Elder Faith, ancestral workings are an integral part of my practice. Technically speaking, every time I commune with my Gods, I'm connecting with my ancestors on many levels, and I find a lot of satisfaction is to be had from working this way. The Tradition that I follow places great emphasis on connecting with the ancestors, and I can't think of a single working that doesn't involve them in some way.

I've been a Pagan for a long time now, since I was 12. To my mother's horror (she was a devout agnostic), I began reading books on Witchcraft. She was terrified that I would follow in the footsteps of my father, who had been a member of a coven and a ceremonial magick lodge in Bristol, England until poor health put a stop to his trips there. In 1983 I joined my first coven, an Alexandrian coven in London, and in 1988 I became High Priest of my own coven in Luton, England, where I followed a predominantly Alexandrian path until 1997, when I moved to Los Angeles.

Somehow, I always knew that while I loved the path I was on, it wasn't the path I would be on for life. I knew there was something deeper within me that would be expressed by a more instinctual way of working, and I found my ancestors - ironically - seven thousand miles from the land that spawned me. I joined Raven's coven in 2000, part of a Tradition that worked with the Welsh Celtic deities of my blood ancestors, and taught the value of 'remembering' ancestral memories and a rich dark shamanic form of practice that felt so true to me. But that's enough background.

Whenever we do a rite, we start by activating the altar. There are two essential things on our altar, the Stone and the Bone. The Stone is our hearthstone - the coven has one, and many if not all of us have personal ones on our own altars too. It represents the hearth at which we gather - a strong family connection. It has other meanings too, but that is the primary one. The Bone is traditionally a skull, and in simpler times would have literally been the skull of an ancestor. For us it is more practical to use a beautiful life-size pewter skull, covered in Celtic knotwork. This represents the Ancestors, and when we activate the altar, part of it is to 'breathe life' into the ancestors, that we may enflesh their legacy. We always invite them to attend our rites, and at our initiations they are an essential component, as the candidate is first fostered into the family, and then later, when the ancestral memories have been shown to be active in them, adopted into the family as full members.

Our training is experiential - we learn by doing, and the exercises we do are designed more to awaken those ancestral memories than they are to teach us technique. We do use technique, but once the memories are awakened, we find that the tools that got us there often fall away to allow the inherent processes to take over. We also seek to expand our understanding of Lore, and that is where tapping the bone comes in. Alongside our practical work, we make use of myth, poetic language and riddles to help us to uncover the underlying principles of our practice, for if we understand the principles, we can devise new or improved practical techniques. Tapping the bone refers to tapping into the ancestral memories in order to work through these mythic, poetic or riddling concepts. It is a form of directed gnosis. The result of this is that the Tradition itself evolves, never static, always changing, as we discover new lore or reclaim lore that was lost.

Each of our initiates works with a Patron/Matron, a specific deity who chose us at our initiation/fostering. We work daily through devotions and meditations to deepen our link with our Patron, and our understanding of the Lore is colored by the nature of that entity. We then share our individual perspectives in order to create a more rounded whole.

Sabbats for us revolve around our path, our Gods, and our ancestors. We do not use an agricultural Wheel of the Year, but rather the cycle of the Sacred King. As a result, we all walk the Wheel in a very real way - it has a profound effect on every aspect of our lives, and our Sabbats flow together as parts of a whole because of this. At Samhain, we work a public rite with Gwyn ap Nudd and the Wild Hunt, bringing the souls of those who died during the year together to be escorted through the Gates into the Cauldron of Rebirth, and a private working, where we explore the Mysteries of the Mound.

Part of our involvement in ancestral working is that we don't hold with the modern concept of reincarnation. We see the rebirth of individuals as a privilege, not a right. Most people when they die are returned to the Cauldron of Cerridwen, to become part of the cosmic 'soup' from which all things are made. Whilst they live again, it is not as one discrete individual, but rather their components are recycled. However, there are those who, by some great deed of heroism, spirituality or wisdom, earn the right to come back as whole individuals. We call them the Mighty Dead, and they become teachers and leaders who come back again and again until they are ready to stop returning. These are the ancestors we work with, and learn from, and hope to become.

One last note on ancestors - believing, as we do, that time only appears to be linear, we see ancestors as being those who came before us, and those who come after us; ancestors who were, and who are yet to be. Working with ancestors requires an appreciation of paradox, for as the old Witch saying goes, 'Truth is most oft found twixt the horns... .'

Generally, books on Wicca don't speak much about ancestral work, and there is an unfortunate popular impression that one of the great differences between Wicca and Traditional Witchcraft is that Wiccans don't work with ancestors. This is not true. It may not be written about much, but from my years as an Alexandrian High Priest, I can tell you that while they work in a different way, the ancestors do play an important part for the Wicca as well. Traditional Witches often put down Wiccans as 'Fluffy Bunnies' because they are generally more inclined to lighter, gentler practices, but Wicca is a tradition as valid as any passed on within a family for generations, and Gardner himself showed evidence of tapping the bone when he wrought his Wicca out of the pieces he was given by his initiators. Likewise, Wiccans often put down Traditional Witches as being dark, even demonic, when the truth is that we all come out of the darkness, and the point of balance is where there is greatest power and beauty. Dark and Light, Black and White, Witches crafting through the Night.

Morning

by Hedgewizard

Today the sun shines on the good and the evil in our world
Today for one moment in the world; light will reign.
In the morning hour of dawn we can touch the Devine
And mime the true nature we all hope to keep alive
Our passion is turned to the dance of ages in love and creation
Our station being as the plants and trees and lilies of the field
All being one with the great spirit of the universe
And all the souls and all the sentries and all the creatures
Bow their knees in thought and silently say as a chant
What a beautiful dawn.

Usage of Animals and Animal Body Parts in Traditional Witchcraft

by Radomir Ristic

The topic about which we are going to talk isn't the most popular one, and often it is very unfairly neglected by many people. Perhaps the reasons for this we could find in an effort to present traditional witchcraft as a little bit milder than actually is, because these things aren't popular in today's society. However, we believe that no one should do something like that. Traditional witchcraft is as it is, and it is our obligation to present it in its true colors.

It is familiar that almost every witch tradition uses animal body parts for performing its rituals. Those are mainly animal horns, bones, claws, hairs, teeth, paws, hide, and skulls of course. Beside those, in ritual also can be used animal blood and internal organs.

If we begin from the start, we can see that this form of witch's practice isn't so brutal like people can imagine when somebody mentions something like that. To avoid confusion we should know that animal sacrificing really exists in Traditional Witchcraft, but that it isn't a mandatory or popular practice, not in any case. To provide a clear explanation we are going to cite an example. In Balkan tradition there is a custom to sacrifice a hen if some person is very ill. It is considered that if destiny couldn't be avoided and that someone must die, people resort to cunning. Namely, a certain person's destiny is traded for the hen's destiny. The ritual is very simple. The Witch takes the hen in her left hand and a hatchet in her right hand and stops near a tree stump. Then she swings the hen in the air several times and after that, she puts it onto tree stump. Before cutting the hen's head off, she recites:

"To chase away death from (name), I am sending it to you."

Although this modest ritual with a humane motive could look brutal to some people, we must bear in mind that the Witch, probably a woman from the village who performed this ritual would probably slaughter that hen anyway to make lunch for her family. It means that this procedure is normal in her environment.

Sacrificing of big animals was usually avoided. Their life mainly was offered to "higher forces" and it was considered those animals anyway would die after that, so people could decide that "higher forces" accepted that sacrifice and, accordingly, whether the performed ritual was successful or not.

When we talk about animal body parts used in ritual practice and their origin, undoubtedly we can say that the Witch procures them in several ways, but according to certain rules. For example, in eastern Serbia we met one male witch who used animal horns and skulls for his rituals. When we asked him from where he got those things, he said that he took horns from a cow that died a natural death, and he took the skull from his donkey that accidentally drowned, hunters who killed a wolf that dashed into the sheepfold gave him its larynx, etc. We weren't able to find any Witch who deliberately killed some animal to be able to use its body parts. Still, we know that this practice exists but only in rare cases. One of them is making a special amulet that the Witch is going to use her whole life, and another is when she kills some bird to make medicine for epilepsy from the bird's blood, or for making a love potion from the bird's heart.

The origin of animal body parts is crucial and that is the thing that determines for which purposes they are going to be used. Lots of attention is focused on the way in which the animal died. If the animal died a natural death, its body parts will be used for positive purposes because it didn't lose its magical power and it didn't suffer while dying. If wolves tore the ram apart, its horns will be used for attacks or so-called "Wars of witches". However, if the ram was prepared for some feast, its horns will be used for positive purposes. If the ram died because of old age or somebody hit it with a car, its skull or horns will be used in rituals with a positive outcome.

Beside the origin of animal body parts, great attention is focused on animal species. Not all animals have the same value and why some of them are more valued then others we can find out from Witchcraft myths and beliefs from a given territory. To avoid talking in a very detailed manner we are going to cite some of the most important things that we found out talking with Witches in the field.

Animal claws and teeth are the most used body parts for making amulets. We are going to mention several. Wolf's tooth, bear's claw, and eagle's claw are used to make amulets for protection. As a rule, these body parts must be topped with silver while pronouncing an incantation. After that, the amulet must be hooked onto a chain or the person must carry it in their pocket. Hunters help the Witch to get these body parts.

Hair from wolves and bears are used for fumigation. People who have problems with panic attacks or some psychical problem must be treated with these. While the person is laying down, Witches use an icon lamp and wave it above the person, pronouncing the appropriate incantation. Hunters also help the Witch to get these animal body parts too.

Animal skulls have different applications in different Traditions. In some regions they could represent the deities of the local system, but not in the Balkans. The skull of a black ram, that died a natural death or was slaughtered for some holiday, could be used to protect from evil. In the early days, people used to place it above the entrance. The right horn of a black ram was used for making a sheath for the kustura (the magical knife).

The skull of a wolf must be used when you want to hurt somebody. Through that skull, you must pour water from some magical spring, so the water flows onto a picture of the person you want to hurt, or onto a doll made of rags from the rubbish heap. Sometimes the picture and doll could be pulled through the wolf's throat or a "zev". A Zev is leather cut from a wolf's jaws and dried, and it represents some sort of magical circle. The purpose of this magic is to take away the strength from a certain person. Hunters help the Witch to get this skull. The skull of a fox also could be used for negative purposes.

The skull of a donkey could be used in similar way, but to make a certain person to lose their mind, to become stupid and dull, unaware of everything that is going on in their vicinity. A Witch procures this skull when an animal is killed or dies.

Horns could be used in several ways. As we mentioned before, from the horns of a black ram was made the sheath for the magical knife – the kustura. For this purpose thehorns of deer and roebuck were also used. The Witch must find these horns in the wood. But horns were also used to make beakers for making potions. They were used as a funnel and the water that runs through them was considered magical. We were lucky to participate in one ritual during which one male Witch poured water from the spring directly into a cow's horn and then used that same water with dogwood to make a liquid for washing one person who was asking for his help. That person needed to wash their face everyday with that water to get rid of bad luck that followed them.

Animal hides were also used for different things. Little drums made of ram's hide were used in rituals in Croatia. The famous torbica-zobnica (Witch's bag) is made of ram's hide. The Witch takes a ram's hide from an animal that is slaughtered for some feast.

In addition to everything else, we should mention that sometimes frog's hide, dried snake, and bat's wings were used. Hides of snake and frog were used in rituals for defense, and bat's wings were used in love magic but as a protection. By custom, the Witch could obtain these animal body parts from road-kill or animals found dead in the wild.

Candlemas and The Land Ceremonies Charm
By R.J. Thompson

Candlemas and Brigid

Where can one begin in relation to this rich subject? I suppose that one would begin with the old festival of Imbolc (also Imbolg and Oimelc,) literally, "ewe's milk," celebrated on February first. This would mark the time when the ewe's were milked at the beginning of spring. It has been suggested by some authors, that the name implies purification, which many of it's rites have included, based upon the theory that the word used to denote milking is derived from an Indo-European root word meaning purification, but I have seen no evidence of this.

Regardless of the origins of this feast day it later became dedicated to the goddess/saint Brigid/Brigid/Bridget/Bride. Brigid was, and is a patron goddess/saint of poetry, the hearth, family, healing, metal-working (thus making her important within smith honoring Craft traditions,) fire, and education. In certain regions she also seems to have held an association with battle, animals and nature in general. It bears mentioning that there have recently been several authors to question her relation to fire. All associations aside, it is somewhat unclear how the goddess/saint became linked with the festival. What we can be sure of, is that she was most certainly associated with the day by the dawn of the modern era.

By the eighteenth and nineteenth centuries tradition held that Brigid would visit the homes of the virtuous on the eve before her feast day. During this time it was customary to place a cloth, ribbon, garment, etc. upon the window-sill overnight to be blessed by the goddess/saint in her passing. Supposedly, this would then protect the wearer from headaches. It was also customary to hold a formal dinner to mark the passing of winter on her feast day. A portion of this feast, often bread or a cake, was placed on the same sill as an offering to the passing goddess/saint. St. Brigid's Crosses were also woven from rushes and hung over doorways or in rafters as a greeting to her on her holy day. These crosses have four equal arms and bear some resemblance to the swastika.

Another custom celebrating Brigid was to dress straw doll in clothing and decorate it with shells, stones, crystals, flowers and jewelry. These decorations would be added to the doll as it was taken in a procession from house to house where homage was paid to it. In some regions the procession was conducted by the young women who would wear all white as a sign of their purity and youth. The elder women would have a bed made, often of straw, for the effigy of the "Bride" next to which a wand made of a "feminine wood" was placed. A chant would accompany this in similar manner to: *"Brigit, Brigit, come over, thy bed is ready," "Bride, Bride, come over and make your bed,"* or *"Bride, Bride, come in, thy bed is made. Preserve the house for the Trinity."* The morning following this celebration the ashes of the fire would be studied to see if the goddess/saint had truly visited the household. If a mark was found, it was a good sign. If no sign of the Bride was seen it was an ill omen. The remedy for such an ill fate was to bury a cock at the crossing of three streams and to then burn incense on the household fire before next laying down to bed.

In England, it should be noted that this day is associated with the stirring of hibernating snakes. A charm against such goes like so:

Today is the day of Bride,
The serpent shall come from the hole,
The queen will come from the mound,
I will not molest the serpent,
The serpent will not molest me.

To the witch there is obvious symbolism found herein. The queen coming from the mound is the resurrection or reincarnation of the spring goddess upon the Earth. The serpent in this instance could be an actual serpent, or on a more esoteric level, symbolize a "second winter." This charm would be a call to the emerging goddess to guard the land against the second winter (or late ending winter) or else protect the petitioner against the fangs of snakes. On a note that will sound closer to home for some traditional crafters, this could also be the queen coming forth as the spring goddess and the serpent representing something more positive, the revitalization of the power of the Land.

In later times these St. Brigid's Day customs were often celebrated in conjunction with the festival of lights, Candlemas, honoring the purification of the Virgin Mary on February second. This day was said to mark the return of Mary to the temple in Jerusalem to be purified after giving birth to Jesus Christ. On Candlemas day, new candles would be blessed upon the high altar in the church. Some of these candles would be burnt before the image of the Virgin, while others were taken home and burnt to protect against storms and sickness. From these customs we get our name "Candlemas." This custom may be traced back to Roman times when people would process through the streets (not unlike the Bride custom) bearing candles and torches in honor of the goddess Februa (namesake of the month February) who was the mother or Mars. This practice was eventually banned by the Church and the custom of lighting candles for the Virgin was thus instated. This was also seen as a time for purifying the self. Brand has this to say of the adaptation of the custom in his *Popular Antiquities:* "he (the Pope) thought to undo this foule use and custom, and turn it into God's worship and that of our Lady's." Somehow this was supposed to have "hallowed" the old Roman festival. There was a particular divination associated with Candlemas night and the held in Ireland. On Candlemas night candles are named after each member of a family and then lit. The first to burn out is the first to die, and so on to the last.

In the northern countries the Anglo-Saxons would give offerings of cakes to their gods during the month of February which they called "Sol-monath" or "Cake Month." I have also seen this festival referred to as "Disting." This custom can be seen in the "Land Ceremonies Charm" of the eleventh century. It bears mention that this could be the origin of the customary leaving a cake or loaf of bread for Brigid. The festival of lights, however, had much appeal upon it's arrival in these northern countries where the winters were quite dark and cold, more so than in Mediterranean Rome.

The whole of the Candlemas celebration was meant to honor the first stirrings of spring, though spring does not always stir at this time of year in the temperate regions of the world. Because of this association, much weather lore has become associated with these days. The most popular bit of lore in my native North America, is that of Groundhog Day. On February second, the legend says, the small groundhog shall emerge from his home in the earth from a long winter of hibernation. If he sees his shadow and flees back into his home, six more weeks of winter are said to follow. If, on the other hand our rodent protagonist does not flee but stays out and about, an early spring will befall us. There is another adage that states:

If Candlemas be fair and clear,
Two winters will you have this year.

Winter on continental Europe may well be on it's way to ending by this time, but in America, it is not always so. Those born in my native Michigan, or on the New England coast can testify that there have been many winters in which fair whether has broken in February only to lead to more harsh blizzards following into the early so called "spring." There is a rhyme which warns the farmer of this "second winter" and have him take the proper precautions:

Half the wood and half the hay
You should have on Candlemas Day.

This is a very true statement in the northern continental states. These fortifications would be very necessary for the early American farmer to survive the foul "second winter" so common to our shores. This weather lore may quite possibly bear a connection to the emergence of the spring goddess or Bride of antiquity!

It is worth mentioning that the festival of lights falls at a time when, although frigid in northern climes, the days begin to become noticeably longer, thus we get the celebration of the waxing light or festival of lights. In many Craft communities this waxing of light heralds the coming of spring and so Candlemas/Imbolc, though still in the heart of winter's bitter cold, marks the beginning of the spring quarter and is marked by the sigil of the five branched stave which represents the hand held up with five fingers raised. In some covens the festival of Candlemas also marks the beginning of the ritual year. In certain variations of the myth of the coming of spring from winter the hag goddess imprisons the maiden goddess of the spring in the late autumn only to find her rescued by a gallant knight when the tide of Candlemas arrives. While in other tales they are the same goddess who grows old in the autumn twilight and is made youthful again at Candlemas by drinking from a well of youth or some other mystical means.

The Land Ceremonies Charm of the Anglo-Saxons

The Land Ceremonies Charm is often quoted or misquoted in modern pagan ritual and magic, though I wonder how many of these would be magicians know the origins of the words that they speak. For any educated pagan, some of the words found within this charm should seem familiar. The charm itself dates back, at least, to the early eleventh century. It may well be that this was a series of separate charms strung together to make one great and impressive ritual. The purpose of the rite would seem to be an assurance that a crop would thrive. Many pagan elements would seem to be present in the rite, though the written variation which survives today is very much a Christian one, going as far as to require a "mass priest" to fulfill certain functions. I will here summarize the rite.

The Land Ceremonies Charm begins by stating that it is a remedy to improve crops and land that will not properly produce, or to remove any ill tidings and bewitchments placed upon the land. It then goes on to state that one should go by night and dig up four tufts of earth, one from each corner of the land to be cured. It then states that honey, oil, milk, and yeast from each beast living upon the land (livestock) and one sprig of each "nameable" plant growing upon the land excepting the buck-bean. Holy water is then to be applied and allowed to drip three times upon the underside of the tufts. Then the practitioner must say: *Grow and multiply and fill the earth,* followed by three *Our Father's*.

Following this the tufts must be taken to a church and the "mass-priest" must sing four masses over the tufts while the green side faces the altar. The tufts are then returned to their places of origin upon the land before the sun sets and one aspen cross is placed beneath each. Upon the four arms of each cross must be written "Mathew, Mark, Luke and John." These crosses are placed in the bottom of each hole and the tufts are placed over them. The words Cross of Matthew... and likewise for each are are uttered over the crosses before placing the tufts over them. Following these steps the words *"Grow, etc..."* are said nine times followed by an equal number of *Our Father's*. Then the practitioner must bow nine times to the east and say:

Eastwards I stand, for favors I ask,
I ask the glorious Lord, I ask the great God,
I ask the Holy Guardian of Heaven,
I ask the earth and heaven above

*and the just, holy Mary
and the heaven's might and the high hall,
that I might be able this charm, by the grace of God
with my teeth intone with fixed purpose
make these crops start growing for our benefit,
fill the earth with firm faith
beautify the surface for the prophet said
that he should have recompense on earth who alms
distributed justly according to the Lord's will.*

Following this the practitioner must turn thrice clockwise then lie down at full length, recite the Litany followed by the Sanctus. Then the Benedicite must be chanted with arms outstretched followed by the Magnificat and the Lord's Prayer, thrice. The land must then be commended to Christ and Mary and to the honor of the land owner.

As if this were not elaborate enough, there is more to follow. An unidentified seed must be taken from "a charity seeker" and paid twice what it is worth. All of the ploughing gear is gathered together and in the wood is inserted the seed, frankincense, fennel, hallowed paste, and hallowed salt. This would take the place of some form of plough blessing. The seed is placed in the body of the plough and is done lastly with the words:

*Erce, Erce, Erce, Mother of Earth
may the Almighty, the Eternal Lord, grant you
fields growing and thriving
increasing and strengthening,
tall stems, fine crops
both the broad barley
and the fair wheat
and all of the crops of the earth.
May God eternal grant
and his saints that are in heaven,
that his crops be protected against any and all enemies,
and be guarded against ills of any kind,
against the sorcery spread throughout the land.
Now I pray the Creator who made the world
that there should be no woman so word-skilled, no man so cunning
as to be able to change the words thus spoken.*

The plough is then driven forth to cut the first furrow while saying:

*Greetings to you, earth, mother of men!
May you be full of growth in God's protecting arms,
filled with food for the benefit of mankind.*

Then meal of each type grown upon the land is taken and a loaf of bread as broad as the palm of a hand is baked, kneaded with mild and holy water and lain in the first furrow. This is then recited:

Field full of food for man,
brightly seeding, you shall be blessed
in the holy name that created this heaven
and this earth that we live on;
may the god who made these grounds grant us the gift of growth
so that for us each grain shall come to fulfillment.

Then the following is said thrice: *Grow in the name of the Father, be blessed. Amen.* Followed by the Lord's Prayer thrice. With this the charm is done.

The pagan and Christian elements are both obvious in the rite, and it is quite likely an old pagan rite later claimed by the Church. One can see by reading this rite how it might be appropriate to the festival of Candlemas and the waxing light. It is only appropriate for such a fertility rite to take place in the dawn of the season of fertility and planting. This was one of my first impressions when I first came into contact with this rite. As such, I have adapted it to use as an agrarian ritual for use within traditional covens at the tide of Candlemas. My adaptations of the rite, as a Candlemas ritual follow.

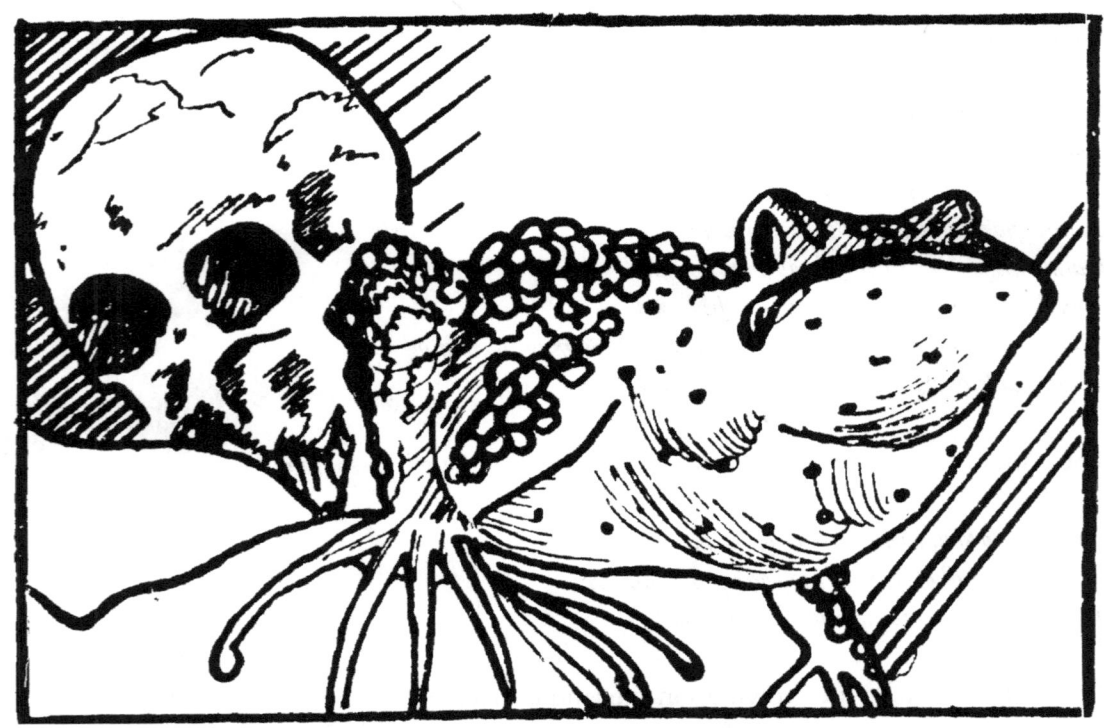

Cosmic Soup and the Mighty Dead
by Peter Paddon

There are a lot of different opinions about reincarnation. Many are loosely based on Hindu and Buddhist beliefs, while others are based on personal insights. One thing that most NeoPagan ideas about reincarnation share is the idea of choosing whether or how you come back. The popular idea seems to be that when Joe dies, he will come back as Joe's spirit in another body. He won't remember being Joe, unless he is sufficiently spiritually enlightened to earn the right to remember, but the Spirit of Joe lives on intact and eternal.

For me, this is a very simplistic interpretation of the Eastern philosophies, and not one I subscribe to at all. Among other things, I do past life regressions, so it usually comes as a surprise to people when they find out that I don't agree with the idea of a linear progression of lives for the individual. So what do I believe in?

First, let me state that I absolutely accept the concept of reincarnation, but for me it is more a case of recycling than the continuation of an individual. You see, my ancestors believed that when you died, you were placed in the Cauldron of Rebirth, and all that you were, body, soul and spirit, returned to the Cosmic soup from which it came. New bodies, spirits and souls were created from this soup, so yes, you reincarnate, you come back, but not as one discreet individual. This has several important ramifications for me. Firstly, it means that the progress of the individual is of vital importance to the progress of humanity as a whole, because when you return to the soup, your level of enlightenment will raise or lower the overall level of enlightenment of the whole soup, just as the flavor of individual ingredients affect the overall flavor and quality of a mundane soup. Secondly, it is not a matter of choice. There is no more choice than there is concerning the breakdown of your physical components to return to the earth, be it by decomposition or by fire.

There are exceptions – the Mighty Dead. My ancestors also believed that there were individuals who became worthy, by acts of heroism, great spirituality, wisdom or leadership, to become one of the Mighty Dead, who do not return to the soup, but emerge from the Cauldron revitalized. These are the Great Teachers and Heroes, and they are rare but essential for the progress of the whole of humanity.

So why do I do past-life regression work, you might ask – well I also believe in ancestral memories. For me, the lives that are tapped into during the regression sessions are those we carry memories of in our blood, our bones, our genetic makeup. I've noticed patterns in the geographical placement of individual's "past lives" that suggest the migration of a family over the eons. This becomes of vital importance in the spiritual path I follow, where the aim is to recover and reconnect to the Lore of our ancestors. This approach has reaped dividends for me and those I work with.

This is also strongly connected to my attitude towards free will and destiny. I don't believe in free will, not because I subscribe to a concept of predestined actions that were set in stone at the beginning of time. I don't think anything is set in stone before it occurs, and all options are always open, but the decision we make at any given moment is the only decision we could make at that moment, for better and worse. Therefore, in the instant, there is no choice, no free will. We are bound to respond the way we do. But awareness of that enables us to overcome it. We cannot be other than who we are in the instant, but we can work to change who we are, so that our reaction is different because we are different. It is not an easy concept to grasp, because it is non-linear, and involves an awareness of the eternal now behind the illusion of Time. Thus we cheat Fate by surrendering to it, and working with it instead of against it. Walking the path of the Craft was never meant to be easy, and much of it involves reconciling apparently irreconcilable points of view, paradoxes. As an old saying goes, the Truth lies "betwixt the horns."

The concept of reincarnation involves paradox too. We are reborn through the Cauldron, but who we are ceases to be. Yet by encountering our death and rebirth whilst still in the body, we can move towards the realm of the Mighty Dead, to ride with Gwyn ap Nudd on the Wild Hunt instead of being that which They hunt, the souls of the recently departed. It all sounds rather melodramatic, but it is just the cycle of life and death. Some Christians make a big deal about being born again, and some Pagan paths talk about being twice-born, but the deeper Mysteries refer to the Greatest among us as Thrice-Born or Thrice-Great, such as Hermes Trismegistus. First we are born of our mother, and then reborn of the Goddess, but that last step is the doozy – to be reborn of the Cauldron while still in the flesh... it takes wisdom, courage, and surrender.

Funnily enough, the concepts upon which the NeoPagan and New Age ideas of reincarnation are built are actually closer to this idea of Cosmic Soup than you might think. Like many spiritual ideas, reincarnation was simplified for the masses by the gurus of the sixties, and the buffet-style spirituality of the 21st century embraces that simplicity. It isn't a bad thing, but there are some who look for deeper, darker fare, and that leads them down avenues that were never meant to be for everyone. To each according to their needs – all paths lead to the same destination, some are just longer, or harder, or take a more scenic route. When all's said and done, in this too, we merely do what we are fated to do... we do what is necessary.

The Rite of Candlemas and the Land Ceremonies Charm
By R.J. Thompson

Ritual preparation: four tufts of Earth must be taken from each quarter of the land to be sained. This is to improve the crop of the following year. These tufts must be gathered, by night, prior to the rite. Oil, honey, yeast and milk must also be present, if these can be taken from the land to be hallowed, all the better. It is also traditional to take a portion of each plant growing on the land, save for buck-bean, but this is unnecessary. Four aspen crosses, Bride's crosses or swastikas must also be made. Four beeswax candles may also be used and buried along side the crosses if it is desired.

The Compass is Drawn as normal

Invocation of the Master

Magister steps forward and rings the bell to the north:

> Master
> I call to you on the crooked path,
> I tread upon the leftway road,
> Searching and calling for You!
> I cal you as a humble servant!
> I call you as a sorcerer!
> I call you as a cunning witch!
> Come forth and feast with your disciples!

Song of the Bride

Ring the bell to the north:

> Today is the day of the Bride
> The serpent shall come from the hole
> The Queen will come from the mound
> I shall not molest the serpent
> The serpent shall not molest me!

Dame (or other woman) steps before the Coven:

> Rejoice! A child is born!

Coven:
>Who has born the child? What is the child's name?

Dame (woman)

>The Love in your hearts has born the child. Her name is Compassion.

Coven

>Then show us the child!

Magister leads the Maid forth (may be represented by some form of corn dolly or cross)

>Behold for She has come, and she shall bring the spring, and blessings onto the fields of the Mother! She was led to us by the watch fire! The Bride shall wed and lay with the King and so bear Him anew! With Her arrival, let the land be renewed!

The Land Ceremonies Charm

Owner of the land anoints the bottoms of the tufts with holy water, allowing the water to drip thrice on the bottom of each, then says over them:

>Grow and multiply and fill the Earth!

Owner then draws three crosses in the air.

The Magister then performs a Hallowing over each tuft by breathing thrice upon each and saying:

>Be consecrated and imbued with the might of the Wanes and Fate's Will and increase and prosper and grow by Moon and Sun and Stars, Earth, Water, Fire, and Sky!

The Magister here blesses each cross (and candle if they are being used) with holy water. He then leads the coven out of the Compass by making a bridge in the east. All walk to the places where the tufts were taken from the Earth, starting in the north. At each quarter a cross (and candle) is placed and the tuft over it. At each the Magister says nine times:

>Grow and multiply and fill the Earth!

And all draw three crosses in the air three times. At the eastern quarter (being the last) the land owner speaks this blessing:

> Eastwards I pray, for favors I ask,
> I ask the Prince of Light,
> I ask the Guardian of the Bridge,
> I ask the Earth and the Sky,
> And the Maid of Spring
> And Hell's might and the hall of Wormsel,
> That I might be able this charm, by Fate's will,
> With my teeth intone, and with fixed purpose
> Make the crops grow, and for our benefit,
> Fill the Earth, and with firm faith
> Beautify the surface that it might be whole.

Then all turn thrice clockwise and (for those who wish and are able) lie at full length while the Magister recites:

> Blessed is the plough, the lover of Earth.
> Blessed be the Tree, Fruit and Seed
> Blessed be the ribbon and all it binds
> Blessed is the sweat of creation
> Blessed are those who toil and use craft
> Blessed forever be Cain's manufacture and work
> Blessed be all that wrest life from the Earth
> Blessed are the servants of the Master
> Fertile shall be the cow and all Kine
> Fruitful shall be the Kine to her young
> Powerful shall be the Bull
> Generation springs from his loins
> Blessings unto all life
> Peace and plenty to all that lives
> Strength and joy to all that is born
> And to that which still awaits
> To all creatures, the Master's help
> Naturals all
> Blessings, food unto all
> May Old Hornie Shepard you all
> Blessed thrice be.

Coven:
> Earth has awakened, Love is afoot again.

All return across the bridge to Hell and back into the Compass. Then take a seed gathered from a "charity seeker" (traditionally) and paid twice it's worth and insert it into the plough (or main gardening tool as the case may be) while the Magister (or Dame) says:

> Erce, Erce, Erce, Mother of the Earth,
> May the Master, the Horned One, grant You
> Fields growing and thriving,
> Increasing and strengthening,
> Tall stems and fine crops,
> Both the broad barley,
> And the fair wheat,
> And all of the crops of the Earth.
> May the Old One grant,
> That Your crops be protected against all and any enemies
> and be guarded against all ills of any kind,
> Against ill sorcery spread throughout the land
> Now I ask favor the of Fate who made the world
> That there be no woman so word-skilled, no man so cunning
> As to be able to change the words thus spoken.

The plough is then taken from the Compass and the Master drives a furrow and says:

> Greetings to you Earth, Mother of men!
> May you be full of growth in Woden's protecting arms,
> Filled with food for the benefit of all humanity.

Take then a cake as broad as the palm of the hand, kneaded with milk and holy water and lay it in the first furrow, and the land owner shall say:

> Filed full of food for mankind,
> Brightly seeding, you shall be blessed
> In the holy name the Wanes
> And this Earth that we live on;
> May the Mother who made these grounds grant us the gift of growth
> So that for us each grain shall come to fulfillment.

Land owner then says thrice:

> Grow in the name of all Wanes, be blessed.

And marks three crosses over the furrow thrice

All then return to the compass

A sacrament of bread and wine, sometimes called a "Housle," is here performed

Ending Declaration:

The Rites of Candlemas are over,
Go now with the blessing of the Maid
And bound to the Horned Master.
The Green shall return to the Earth,
She shall feed Her children!

The Compass is swept away and implements retrieved.

Bibliography

Aspects of Anglo-Saxon Magic – Bill Griffiths – Anglo Saxon Books

Folklore of American Weather – Eric Sloane – Hawthorne Books Inc.

Irish Cures, Mystic Charms, & Superstitions – Lady Wilde – Sterling Publishing Co. Inc.

Practical Magic in the Northern Tradition – Nigel Pennick – Thoth Publications

Runic Astrology – Nigel Pennick – Aquarian Press

The Sacred Ring – Michael Howard – Capall Bann Publishing

Secrets of East Anglian Magic – Nigel Pennick – Capall Bann Publishing

The Origins of Popular Superstitions and Customs – T. Sharper Knowlson – Newcastle Publishing Co.

The Stations of the Sun – Ronald Hutton – Oxford University Press

Witchdom of the True – Edred Thorsson – Runa-Raven Press

Unless otherwise stated, all text in within this article is original and Copyright © 2008 by R.J. Thompson. All images used in this document are in the public domain.

Blacksmith as Magus

by Radomir Ristic

Since ancient times, blacksmithing has aroused the interest of people. The invention of metallurgy and the blacksmith's trade marked a transition of ancient humanity to a new technological level. People who know the secrets of blacksmithing have advantages over the ones who didn't know those secrets.

From this historical viewpoint, it is very hard to imagine that sometimes the knowing of those secrets could mean that certain nation have invincible armies, that can build unseen buildings, that can till the soil faster and better from others, etc.

According to all the world myths, the secrets of blacksmithing were transferred to people by deities. In the Book of Enoch, Azazel the archangel did that and consequently he was brutally punished like the Greek Prometheus, who brought fire to his people. In many of today's Witch Traditions those deities are worshipped. It is not very hard to find out why. Two things are crucial here. First of all is the fact that all deities who are protectors of the blacksmith's trade are also chthonic and secondly, all chthonic deities are protectors of magic. Because of these two facts, they are encompassed as subjects of cults. One of the most famous deities of that type is Tubal Caine of the Old Testament.

Beside that, everywhere in the world blacksmiths were always considered to be mages. They had guilds that have many similarities to magical associations of a witchy character. Accordingly, they were considered to be sorcerers and alchemists, and people went to them for help, but were also afraid of them. The basic reason for this fear is the belief that they work together with chthonic forces, or demons, and the Devil himself. In other words, after the arrival of Christianity, old pagan deities - especially ones with chthonic character - were considered to be demons or the Devil. Because of that, the blacksmith was tabooed often and people would avoid having to perform this trade. In Serbian tradition, the blacksmith's trade was invented by the Devil and he gave it to the Serbian people, and the water mill too. Accordingly, blacksmiths became his representatives.

In Serbia, the whole blacksmith shop was considered to be a temple. The anvil, having the role of an altar, was hammered ritually on Saturday, after midnight, in the time of the full moon. Nine naked blacksmiths would hammer it in silence, getting along by using gestures and mumbling. Beside that, thepresence of women was forbidden. The anvil worked in this way becomes a very magical altar.

Petar Z. Petrovic, the ethnologist, shows us to what extent this altar was sacred by retelling an anecdote where one young man walked into the blacksmith's shop and sat down on the anvil. When he looked at the astounded face of the blacksmith he realized than what he just did. He jumped up, worshipped the anvil, kissed it and asked forgiveness from the owner. This demonstrates that common people were aware of the anvil's "sanctity".

The anvil was equated with Bible. In particular, people used to take oaths by putting their hand on the Bible or the anvil, which means they had the same value. The cult of the anvil reaches its height on the day before Sunday or some very important holiday, like Christmas. People used to place wax candles on it, and blacksmiths would pray next to their anvil. At Christmas people used to pour wine on it and that represented offering a sacrifice.

Besides the blacksmith's trade, blacksmiths would practice magic too. Rituals of magical healing were performed on the anvil. Pregnant women used to put around their waist a chain made by the naked blacksmith very late at night, so she could protect itself and her child too. Blacksmiths made amulets too. Some of them were made from a dead mare's horseshoe. Probably the most interesting thing is the fact that all blacksmiths from the Alps, to Bohemia, through Balkans and to south Caucasus had to hit over the anvil on a certain day. They believed that they were strengthening the chain with which the Devil is chained by this ritual. In Serbia, this ritual was performed on the day before Christmas.

Celtic Nine Poems
by Peter Paddon

A Nine poem is an interesting literary device. Basically, you have a poem that has another poem hidden within it, and a third poem hidden within the second. They make powerful invocations, and their creation is an act of meditation and magick.

The Rules

1. The first poem contains hidden within it a second poem, composed of every ninth letter from the first poem.

2. The second poem contains hidden within it a third poem, composed of every ninth letter from the second poem.

3. The number of letters in each poem must be a multiple of nine.

4. The poems do not need to rhyme.

5. Do not count spaces.

How to Do It

1. Start with the third poem. It can be just nine letters long, or a multiple of nine letters.

2. Once you have your third poem, draw out a grid nine wide by the number of letters in the third poem long. For example, if you chose "Sacred One" as your third poem, which is nine letters long, you would draw a 9x9 grid.

3. Write the letters of the third poem down the right-hand column of the grid. Do not leave spaces between the words.

4. Work out your second poem by writing one letter in each square of the grid, making sure the existing letters from the third poem are incorporated, and leaving no spaces. Use a pencil - you'll be doing a lot of correcting...

5. Once the second poem is complete, draw out a fresh grid, 9 wide by the length of the second poem. If you started with the example above, your initial 9x9 grid gives you 81 letters, so your new grid would be 9x81.

6. Write the letters from your second poem in the right-hand column of the new grid.

7. As in 4 above, work out your first poem by writing one letter in each square of the grid, making sure the existing letters from the second poem are incorporated, and once again, leave no spaces.

8. Once the first poem is complete, rewrite it out as an actual poem, with spaces between the words, and divide it up into lines and stanzas. As this is a prose poem, you do not need to try to create a meter or stanzas of equal length - split it into lines and groups of lines as feels right - but try to get the total number of lines to be a multiple of nine.

If you want to, you can do the same with the second and third poems, or you can let the reader work them out for themselves.

What follows is an example that I wrote after carrying Sacred King for my coven one year...

Sacred King

Solitude, exiled I live, apart -
The one Bearer of their story
I follow in the robe of a sacred avatar,
Far from the tumult of sturdy shrouded companions
Who bear the load with me.

Rites to turn on the Wheel,
Taking me along far and Wide,
Hand upon my heart and
Wounded or burdened with
Woe for my callow folk,
Long to walk, and weighty my load.

The Lady sates my need,
Swollen breast feeds my body
As I forge my different parts
To play trickster.

Sudden moisture,
From the clouds that dog
My lonely path,
Now flows toward a tear
From my oracular manner.

I awake defiant -
Fear is gone as I lift
My baggage and continue,
crying out victorious,
For I have visions of
Scattered people who
Affect to be one People reunited.

The power of each word
Arranged to wield
An otherworld meaning
Cannot be ever erased,
For victory is easy
And War is undone when
The Unholy becomes sacred
And the King expires to
Validate aeons of Fear.

Peter Paddon, 2001

As I Will It, So Mote It Be… Or Not.
by Ann Finnin

Every now and again, someone shows the incredible lack of good sense and asks me to teach a Wicca 101 class. After 35 years in the Craft -- 30 of those years running a coven -- it's fascinating to get up in front of a dozen or so people sitting on the edge of their chairs thinking that they have a clue about what they're getting into. Of course, none of them want to spend any time on the history and philosophical underpinnings of Wicca. They all want to get on to the Good Stuff.

"So," I ask, "you guys want to do magic, do you?" Heads nod. A couple of my initiates who are hanging out in the back of the room roll their eyes. They know what's coming.

"Okay," I say, "how do we do a magic spell?" Hands go up. We get the right candles and incense. Check. We cast a circle. Absolutely. We invoke the Goddess and God. Mmmkay. We don't go into just which goddess and god we are invoking and why are we invoking them. That's another lecture.

"So, now what?" Well, now we light the candles and ask the Goddess to give us what we want.

"Whoa Nellie," I say. "Are you guys doing a spell or saying a prayer?" Well, a spell is a prayer, isn't it? Nope. A spell is a spell and a prayer is a prayer. The two are very different. Huh? Brows furrow in confusion. How so?

Here's how so. What you're actually doing in the above 'spell' is not a whole lot different from what you would do if you were a devout Catholic who goes into a church, lights a votive candle in front of the statue of the Virgin Mary and asks Her to grant you something you want -- a job, a lover, a new house, money, whatever. Just because you are making Sacred Space yourself rather than having the church do it for you is immaterial. You are asking Divinity to do something for you rather than doing it for yourself.

Oh, but what if what I want isn't good for me, or isn't right? What if it means that someone else has to suffer? Won't I incur Bad Karma if I just demand it? Ah there, as they say, lies the rub.

In order to avoid such ethical conundrums, many books on Wicca recommend that when doing a spell one should recite something called the Karmic Clause.. This is a phrase that you tack on to the end of your spell which goes something like: 'this or something better for the highest good of all concerned.' This proviso is supposed to insure that whatever you ask for is free of the above Bad Karma since presumably the Goddess will only give you what is right and good for you to have and harms nobody in the process.

However, this Karmic Clause begs a number of very important questions. If you're demanding something that's bad for you and/or not right, why are you demanding it? If you don't know whether or not something is right or good for you, why aren't you cultivating that inner awareness that will tell you in No Uncertain Terms if something is right or good for you? And if somebody else has to suffer in order for you to have what you want, is it really worth having?

The fallacy here is that there actually is 'good' or 'bad' karma. Karma simply is a word that means 'consequences.' Everything we do or don't do, magically or otherwise, has consequences, both pleasant and unpleasant. When we perform a spell, we knock a cue ball into a rack of other balls, sending them every which way. Some will go into the pocket and some won't. That's the chance we take when we do a spell. Now if we are wise, we will learn the laws of physics governing the trajectory of the balls and use that information to determine where best to strike the cue ball and with what force. But, once we've done that to the best of our ability, all we can do is to hit the ball and deal with the results whatever they are. Or, not shoot pool. Period.

What the so-called Karmic Clause is advocating, pure and simple, is an abdication of responsibility for one's actions. When a witch makes the commitment to do a spell, he or she should consider all of the possible repercussions before even beginning the ritual. What exactly needs to be done and why? What might the results be? Is the desired outcome good, or merely pleasant? Is it right? If not, are there any extenuating circumstances that might indicate that it should be done anyway? Will someone suffer because of it? If so, should one consider the outcome worth the 'collateral damage' or refrain from doing the spell altogether?

Difficult questions, these. But you must answer them honestly for yourself before you decide to do the spell in the first place. And the Goddess (or the God, or the gods, or the elementals, or the archangels, or whoever else you invoke) isn't going to step in and rescue you from any unpleasantness that results from your decision. That's the difference between a spell and a prayer, between religion and magic. If you are to be a witch or a magician, you have to take the rap yourself for whatever it is that you set in motion. Sometimes it will be worth it. Sometimes it won't. But you alone are responsible for whatever happens. You decide what result you want and what consequences you're willing to endure to get it. Then, after all that, you go for it and damn the torpedoes.

Then, and only then, can you say 'As I will it, so mote it be.' And mean it.

Walking the Crooked Path
by Peter Paddon

There are so many arguments going on at any given moment about the differences between Wicca and Witchcraft. Part of the problem is that everybody has their own definition of those two terms. For myself, I know I'm not Wiccan, because I used to be - it is the easier of the two to define, anyway. But the word Witchcraft is harder to nail down, running the gamut from another word for Wicca, through the pre-Gardnerian Mystery Traditions to a practise or way of life unconnected with any specific religion.

My personal practice has led me to stop using the word witch... mostly. Sometimes it is easier to use it to avoid a drawn-out explanation. I prefer the term Cunning Man these days, as what I practise is called the Cunning Art. It is also known as the Crooked Path.

The tradition I initiated (fostered/adopted) into was, at the time, referring to itself as a Family Tradition. This doesn't mean that all rites were PG and kids took part, but rather that the Tradition had been maintained by a family, and entry into the Tradition was by birth, marriage or adoption. I quickly learnt that this was not technically true - although the Magister of the Tradition claimed such a lineage, he was not teaching us the Tradition of his Family, but rather a Tradition based upon, but different than, the one he learnt from his parents.

I have recently come to believe that there is no such thing as a Family Trad in the accepted sense of the term, and the term itself is these days a source of riducule in many circles. What I do believe is that there are families who retained pieces of the puzzle, certain practices or lore that were handed down without a complete understanding. There are those who seek to reconstruct these fragments into a whole, and that is what I believe I initiated into.

My own practice continues this reconstruction, through a combination of research and what we call "tapping the bone", recovered ancestral memories. So what does the Crooked Path entail?

First and formost, the Crooked Path involves working with Ancestors, both to recover lore and praxis, and to empower the crafting that we do. We believe that in the nonlinear "now" of sacred space, ancestors are both before us and behind us, past and future. Our interactions with our Gods are quite different from many Wiccan and Pagan paths, as we see the Gods through multiple facets, as aspects, archetypes, individuals, parts of ourselves, and special ancestors, all at the same time. Our path is filled with paradox, and it is the balanced resolution of these paradoxes that enable us to grow and evolve spiritually.

Our sacred space is created by laying the Compass Rose. It serves the same effective purpose as casting a circle, but it is so much more, because it is a framework upon which we hang our Lore and our Crafting. It is also known as the Witches' Walk, laying the Moat, the Bloody acre, and the Furrowed Land. It is an interacting with the Land, symbolic and/or actual, and is almost impossible to describe without a practical demonstration.

We work Northern Quarters rather than the Golden Dawn elemental system, and while the names are shared, the "elements" are not the Elements of the GD. Fire in the East, Earth in the South, Water in the West and Air in the North, the "elements" actually refer to qualities of light, and are not fixed in the quarters they are called in. We also work Heights and Depths, and the whole thing exists within the Three Realms, which can be seen as Earth, Sea and Sky, or Heaven, Here and Hel. Everything is connected via the Bile Tree in the center.

Our crafting takes many forms, the Mill and the Cone, the Fetch, the Bale Fire, the Witches' Ladder and others. Our tools are the Stang and the Cauldron, the Hearthstone and the Bone (skull). We have knives for cutting and carving, but do not tend to use them in crafting other than as practical tools. The besom is another important tool.

Instead of the Rede, we have a simple Ethic, best described in the words of Robert Cochrane of the Clan of Tubal Cain: "Do not do what you desire; do what is necessary."

And that Crooked Path we walk upon? Ahead it twists and turns like the back of a serpent, and behind us it is bent like the path through a maze, but beneath our feet it is the Old Straight Track, and thus we walk it, by a bent line, by a straight line, by a crooked line.

There is no reason for this article, beyond the desire to give you a taste of another "flavor" of Paganism. And to express my love for the Path I walk.

Turning the Hand of Fate
by Raven Womack

Turning the Hand of Fate is one way in which I have heard the practice of the cunning arts described. There are definitely many that take this statement very literally. There are those that see Fate as some sort of an unyielding entity or dark power that has preordained all things including how and when each of us will die. Adherents to this school of thought would have us believe that by "Turning the Hand of Fate" we might well be sealing our own fate in the process.

The idea of predestination or preordination is a very old one. The theological definition is basically that God or the Divine if you will has foreordained all things. John Calvin and St. Augustine of Hippo believed that the salvation and damnation of all humans was preordained by God. This is a theological philosophy that has influenced many sects of Christianity through out history. On the surface at least, this seems like a very poor way to convince people to be good since it's all already worked out by God. Why struggle against sin since God's already made up His mind? Then again I am no scholar of Christian thought or theology.

While these two versions of fate or foreordination are similar, they are not exactly the same. For the Christian that believes in predestination that's that, there's no arguing with God. For the crafter that believes in predestination there is the chance to bargain with Fate for a more desirable outcome. That a "deal" can be struck with this dark and resolute power but breaking a deal such as this will have the direst of consequences.

I recently read a book wherein the author describes a very crafty and cunning way to affect the healing of an ill person. The author lost me though when he went on to caution that if the illness and impending death was actually "fated" then the person who facilitated the healing by craft and conjure could in fact be required to pay with their own life to satisfy the debt for cheating Fate. Conversely, he went on to explain that another possibility was that healing the dying person only to forfeit your own life could actually be the "fated" outcome.

The way I see it, this school of thought, makes no sense at all. As a crafter I do realize that everything has a price and everything has a consequence. If we are honorable and respectful in our arts then we will be careful to acknowledge the powers that we work with, conjure and coerce to aid us in our ways and we will pay for them accordingly. Seldom is the price for our craftings more complicated than a few well thought out offerings. If we have to worry about forfeiting our life every time we craft or conjure to heal the sick then it becomes a bit like playing magickal chicken.

I simply do not believe in some unseen and unyielding entity that will only be sated by taking a life in exchange for the one that has been saved. This superstitious babble seems to be designed to make the crafter seem more important than he or she is. As if at every attempt to heal we are putting ourselves in mortal danger thereby masking the healer in a veil of mystery and importance due to the inherent danger involved in attempting the healing. Hogwash! Sure there are times that healing work can take a toll on the healer but any healer worth their salt knows this and prepares accordingly.

The other reason this school of thought seems ludicrous to me is that if I have to worry at every turn whether or not my actions are but the foreordained mastery of the dark and shadowy Fate to bring about my demise then I might as well give up now. For that matter I might as well give up on life in general. In case anybody hasn't noticed life is always just a breath away from being over. Perhaps I should ponder whether or not to cross the street, lest Fate wants me to cross the street so that some speeding bus can come around the corner and squish me. How do I know whether or not a limb from the oak tree in my yard might not break off suddenly and smash into my bedroom killing me, as Fate has preordained.* We simply can not live in fear of "Fate" and be productive human beings not to mention being productive cunning folk.

So, having said all of that, I must say that I do believe that sometimes, someone is supposed to die. I do not claim to know why per se, just that I accept that sometimes the will of the gods is such. I realize that not all crafters or cunning folk are religious but I am. I believe in real and living gods that have a will that is beyond
me to know or understand. Rooted in that belief is the knowledge that in their infinite wisdom it may be their will that someone die or even that some other important or even seemingly inconsequential will take place. In following with that belief is the fact that no matter how crafty or cunning I am I can not thwart the will of the gods. While it is true that there are many in this world that make it a habit to shake their fists at the Gods it is as useless as it is pitiful. So, while I do not believe in the forever insatiable Fate I do believe that sometimes things are just meant to be. However powerful Fate may be, it apparently can be cheated. The Gods on the other hand can not so I need not live in fear of cheating them and paying with life.

In my opinion and experience, fate is truly nothing more than cause and effect. When we choose to take an action there will be some consequence for that action. The actions that we take and the consequences of those actions may be affected by certain probabilities and likely hoods but nothing is predestined. As crafters I believe we must live in a world of infinite possibilities. If we do not, then much of what we seek to manifest is impossible. The end result can not be determined until the action that is to cause the end result takes place and any number of things can effect whether the action will ever take place. Once the action does take place any number of things can affect the probable outcome.

Cunning folk, at least in my opinion should never accept the concept of a totally preordained fate. To accept it is to be bound and ruled by it. I will not be bound by some fear of punishment for upsetting the preordained order of things nor will I accept the idea that there is nothing that I can do to change the outcome, no matter how probable it may seem, of any given situation. That flies in the face of being cunning or crafty, doesn't it?

That being said I know that there will be those of you who will want to split hairs so I will admit that there will always be the possibility of those situations that are totally beyond our control or manipulation. Yes, if you throw me off of the Empire State Building then I would have to admit that the outcome is preordained or fated. On the other hand it is not preordained that I will ever go to the Empire State Building. As I have already mentioned, I also accept the fact that the possibility exists that what ever outcome that I am working towards will be a mute point if it goes against the will of the Gods.

Karma, although an Eastern philosophy is in truth a type of predestination, yet still in keeping with the philosophy of cause and effect. A person's Karma is the rewards and/or punishments that a person will receive in the next life as a result of how they live this life. I am not versed enough in the Eastern religions to know whether or not Karma can be cheated but what I do know is that each person is responsible for their own Karma so I tend to doubt that it can be. In essence the hand that slaps your face is your own; the only way to stop the slap is to not do whatever it is that requires you to be slapped.

Wyrd is often defined in regular mundane dictionaries as fate or sometimes fate personified. It is not surprising that a non-magickal dictionary would get it wrong but then again I have known many magickal people that seem to hold this very same misconception. There are definitely those that believe that the concept of the Norns (alternately called the Fates) weaving a person's Wyrd to be a sort of Northern European Pagan version of the Calvinistic Christian ideas about foreordination but I submit that they are confused and have not really explored the mysteries of Wyrd. The truth of the weaving sisters is that they are constantly weaving. Certainly many things influence how we will act in any given situation but at any time we may act against our nature or in some other way change the pattern that is being woven. We have been given the gift of free will but if all is preordained then free will is useless. The threads that the sisters weave are made up of our ancestry, our personal history and our upbringing, the influences that affect us and the decisions that we make. While it is true that we can not change that which has already happened it is also true that which is yet to happen has not yet been woven and the weaving can not be finished until the life is ended.

Not surprisingly, the philosophy of the Wyrd is in my opinion the only rational philosophy of the crafter. Any person's fate is of course influenced by their upbringing, their ancestry and the effects of their past choices and experiences. A person's fate or Wyrd is simply the likely outcome based on past and current behavior combined with current situations and influences all moving towards a probable outcome, probable but not preordained.

The key is to know that infinite possiblities are within our reach. Sure knowing the probability can be a useful thing, but being bound by it is not in keeping with the cunning ways. Where would we be as a species if we were bound by what was probable? At any given moment we can change our Wyrd with a thought or a word just as the Wyrd of humanity has been spun on a dime by the dreams of forward thinking individuals.

As fate is nothing more than the probable outcome or consequence then yes as cunning folk we can indeed turn the hand of fate. As the nimble fingers of the Wyrd sisters work the threads, the pattern that they weave is guided by our thoughts, words and actions. It is free will that gives all humans the ability to change the future and as cunning folk we have at our disposal all the more tools with which manifest change and thereby *Turn the Hand of Fate*.

Not only can we turn the hand of fate but we should shed the binding fear of interfering with the way things are meant to be that seems to grip so many practitioners today. The ever invasive dread that by using our craft that we may be upsetting the *greater good* inhibits the craft in an insidious way that I find maddening. There seems to be this tendency to overcomplicate and over think even the simplest of craftings. If you are ethical, honorable and respectful in your ways then you need never fear that the dark looming hand of fate will snatch you up for your crafting.

It's really very simple if you think about it but then again I am a simple cunning woman and I have seen all too often the folly of making something more complicated than it has to be.

Besides, if something is truly fated or preordained to happen then we can not change it. By definition it is impossible for us to change that which is foreordained due to the inference of divine foreordination is it not? If the Gods have truly preordained this person or that to die from an illness then regardless of how cunning we are we can not thwart that will. If everything that has happened or is happening or will happen is the product of some divine foreordination then what reason have we to study the cunning arts or even to live for that matter. It makes no sense that cunning folk would believe such a thing.

In the strictest terms, I do not believe that we can "cheat fate." Fate is not a being or entity it is simply a way of expressing the idea that if we continue on a certain path then we will probably experience a certain outcome. Now if for whatever reason the Gods my people swear by, will a certain thing to happen even someone's death, then there is no way that I, or any other crafter, can thwart that will. Unlike those who are constantly shaking their fists at the gods, I do not believe that I can thwart the will of the gods. So even if you were to make the assertion that the will of the gods is fate, I submit that no human, no matter how great a crafter they might be, can thwart the will of the gods.

That leaves the question then do we and can we as crafters actually turn the hand of fate? Yes of course we can and of course we do. We often call upon our abilities and our arts to change the course of things. Like if someone is sick we work to make them well. This does not mean that we work against some invisible entity that has laid out the future for us. It simply means that we work to create the outcome that we need or desire.

Turning the hand of fate is as simple exercising free will. As crafters it is common for us to use our arts to change the way things are going or to change the probably outcome of any given situation. If a person has cancer then we might use our craft to try and heal that person but we should do so without fear of reprisal for being successful in our workings.

I do not understand this fear of working for what you desire. Recently a woman I know asked that our community send energy to her ailing mother. She had recently been diagnosed with a type of cancer after beating another type of cancer only recently. She asked not for healing energy but just for comforting energy in case the healing energy might actually work and thwart the way things are supposed to be. I say that if her mother is supposed to die then die she will and no amount of our interference will change that but if there is a chance to heal her mother then take that chance. It's like some perverted Pagan form of Christian Science philosophy. Christian Scientists don't get medical care because they feel that any illness or disease is God's will. This has resulted in countless court cases against parents that have withheld vital and lifesaving medical service to their children and rightly so. To withhold medical care from a child because you believe it is God's will is reckless and arrogant. It implies knowledge of the will of God and it implies that anything that God can manifest, man can thwart. Now I am in no way accusing this delightful woman of being reckless or arrogant I simply believe she is the product of reckless and arrogant teachers

In the myth of Arianhrod and Llew we find a perfect example of destiny and fate. Llew, Arianhrod's son is "destined" to be the Sacred King by virtue of His divine birth and magickal upbringing yet it is not written in stone. He must accomplish certain things before he can prove that he is worthy of claiming that birth right. If he does not do so then he can not be the Sacred King. If at anytime he decides not to do all that is required of him or if he is unable to the things that are required of him, he will not be sacred King. Now one could argue that once he takes on that role that he fated to die and I would agree with that argument to a point. I would argue that death is the consequence for accepting the mantle of the Sacred King. By accepting that mantle or role if you will, he is basically signing a contract to die at the end of the cycle. Whether that death is to be taken literally or figuratively is a subject for a different time. The death of the Sacred King is simply the end result of becoming the Sacred King, cause and effect.

Making a Traditional Witches' Besom
by Peter Paddon

> The DVD of Making A Traditional Witches' Besom is available from Amazon and from Pendraig Publishing, with an extra hour of history and Lore for just $29.95

For several years I scoured the internet and craft books, looking for instructions on how to make a real besom, as used in British Traditional Crafting. I never found more than a hint here, a snippet there... what information does exist online is about making brooms with broomcorn or straw. So I took my life and memories of a besom-making demonstration from a fair fifteen years ago, and gave it my best shot.

Despite it being my first attempt, it came out very well, and I had the foresight to videotape it, and have my wife take photos. So here it is, for the first time in print: how to make a real traditional witches' besom or broom...

Start with two handfuls of birch twigs at least three feet long. I got mine from a place that supplies them for wreath-making. Traditionally, you would grip them in the jaws of the vice on your broom horse, but I don't have one... so I'm 'gripping' them with 14-inch cable ties from my local computer store (Fry's)

Here I've put my cable ties on (one at the end, and one either side of where I'm going to bind with the willow. The strip of stuff in my hand is a willow withie, obtained online from a basket-weaving supply store. The withies have been soaking in a bucket of water for at least 48 hours.

My lovely assistant, Karen, holds the end of the withie tight while I wrap it around the birch. Do at least three full wraps, and make sure you catch the end you started with under at least one of the wraps.

When your three wraps (or more) are complete, take your bond poker and shove it under the wraps to create a channel through which you pass the end of the withie. Do this two or three times. The bond poker is - in this case - a piece of copper pipe that I removed half of for a few inches, so it has a concave 'blade'. Traditionally it was made from the thigh-bone of a goose.

Here wrap one is completed, and I'm starting in wrap two. Rural tradition has two withie or wire wraps, but this is for Cunning folk, so I'm doing three.

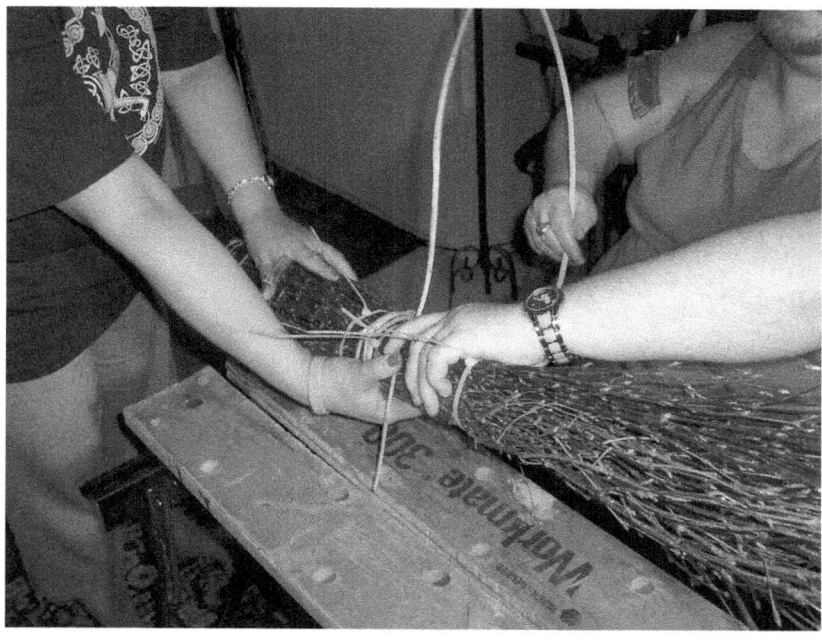

Once again, the bond poker let's me poke the end of the withie under the wrapped part, in order to create a knot. I generally pass the end under the wraps twice, then pass it through the first one that "wraps around the wraps" in order to create a sort of knot. Then I pass it under the wraps once more so I can cut it off where it pokes out from underneath.

Another shot of passing the end through the bond poker, just to make sure you've got the idea.

After cutting the excess from the last wrap, it is time to remove the cable ties and see if my workmanship holds true...

... lucky me, it holds. Not bad for a first attempt, eh?

Now the fun part - trimming the top of the brush. Traditionally, a machette-type blade is used, or in some areas, an axe. Having neither, and failing miserably with the pruning shears, I resorted to power tools. I ended up using my chainsaw, but I don't have a picture of that, as I needed all hands to hold everything steady while I used two hands to control the chainsaw - if I'd had a table saw, it would have done a neater job.

Having survived the making of the broomhead, I take a nice piece of ash, which I have already ground to a point with a belt sander. Once again, a departure from tradition, where I should have whittled it with my knife, but the sander was quicker. By the way, when you are using a natural ash branch rather than a dowell (yuck!), the narrower end is the one that you turn the point on.

Carefully place the point in the center of the nicely cut birch, and once you have gently pushed the head on enough to hold its position, bang it down on the stick so the point is driven well into the head. You are aiming to have the ash pass through all three willow bindings.

If you kept everything nice and tight, the added tightness of inserting the stick will ensure the head stays on. If you are not sure, then before you attach the head, drill a hole in the stick so you can insert a wooden dowell or a horseshoe nail into it through the birch to make sure it stays put. Mine didn't need that, it is on to stay.

And there you have it, the finished besom, crossed with the temporary one we're replacing with it (thanks, Steve, for the old one), along with our stang and cauldron. The lovely Karen, my assistant for that day, had just completed her course of treatment for breast cancer. Unfortunately, she died in September 2007, and is deeply missed.

Current and Soon-To-Be-Released titles from
PENDRAIG PUBLISHING
www.pendraigpublishing.com

The Horn of Evenwood
by Robin Artisson
Available

The Raven's Flight Book of Incense, Oils, Potions & Brews
by Raven Womack
Available

The Forge of Tubal Cain
by Ann Finnin
Available

Sorgitzak: Old Forest Craft
by Veronica Cummer
Available

ALSO COMING SOON

Anatomy For Holistic Therapists
by Dr. Colin Paddon

Balkan Traditional Witchcraft
by Radomir Ristic

The Flaming Circle
by Robin Artisson

Hedgerider
by Eric Cuijpers

The Crooked Path
by Peter Paddon

Egyptian Mysteries
by Peter Paddon

New from PENDRAIG Publishing
Spellcrafting DVDs with Peter Paddon

Craftwise Vol 1: Candle Magick

Author and Witch Peter Paddon teaches the basics of Spellcrafting, and explores the art of Candle Magick. What is Magick and Spellcrafting? The subtle art of Creative Visualization The use of will in spellcasting Candle Magick: Theory of color/candle magick Preparing your candle Working with one candle or many Custom candles Money spell Job spell Healing spell

Craftwise Vol 2: Cord Magick

Author and Witch Peter Paddon teaches the basics of Spellcrafting, and explores the art of Cord Magick. *Knotting the thread of Fate *The ethics of Binding *Traditional forms of knot magick *Protection spell *Travel spell *Justice (legal) spell

Craftwise Vol 3: Talismans

Author and Witch Peter Paddon teaches the basics of Spellcrafting, and explores the art of Talismans. Signs and Sigils AO Spare and the Power of Sigil Magick Materials Spell to get a book Spell to find a house Spell to improve yourself

Craftwise Vol 4: Herb Magick

Author and Witch Peter Paddon teaches the basics of Spellcrafting, and explores the art of herb magick. Incense and brews Mojo bags Poppets and Fith Faths Healing spell Learning spell Spell to break a habit

Craftwise Vol 5: Oils and Crystals

Author and Witch Peter Paddon teaches the basics of Spellcrafting, and explores the art of oils and crystals. Magical uses of essential oils Choosing crystals Cleansing and charging crystals Using rocks and jewels Essential oil spell for enhancing Sight Crystal healing spell Crystal truth spell

Making a Traditional Witches' Besom

Apart from the cauldron, the broomstick or besom is the tool most associated with Witches in myth and fairy tale. Modern witches use the besom too, and in this DVD Peter Paddon - author and Witch - takes a look at the history and Lore of the besom. Then his class turns practical as he looks at the tools and materials needed to make a birch besom and demonstrates exactly how to do it. Peter Paddon is the author of two books on the Egyptian Mysteries: "The Book of the Veil" and "Through the Veil" published by Capall Bann. He is also the creator of the Craftwise series of spellcrafting DVDs, and runs a small company of modern Cunning Folk.

The Sight: Getting It, Using It, Dealing With It

The Sight - the ability to see realms beyond the physical and interact with otherworldly spirits. Join Peter Paddon, author and Witch, as he explores the lore and practise of seership, and demonstrates practical exercises to develop this gift.

DVDs retail at $29.95
www.pendraigpublishing.com

www.ingramcontent.com/pod-product-compliance
Lightning Source LLC
Chambersburg PA
CBHW081502040426
42446CB00016B/3359